I DISSENT

RUTH BADER GINSBURG MAKES HER MARK

For Ruth Bader Ginsburg, whose work and example have paved the way for so many of us, and in memory of Jutta Salzberg Levy, my mother and own personal way-paver
—D. L.

To my mom and dad
—E. B.

Acknowledgments
I am grateful to Justice Ruth Bader Ginsburg for helpful comments on the manuscript that became this book. Thanks as well to Tony Mauro, doyen of Supreme Court reporters, for his review and suggestions. And thank you to my agent, Caryn Wiseman, and my editor, Kristin Ostby, for their enthusiasm for RBG in general, and for this book in particular.
—D. L.

SIMON & SCHUSTER BOOKS FOR YOUNG READERS
An imprint of Simon & Schuster Children's Publishing Division
1230 Avenue of the Americas, New York, New York 10020
Text copyright © 2016 by Debbie Levy
Illustrations copyright © 2016 by Elizabeth Baddeley
All rights reserved, including the right of reproduction in whole or in part in any form.
SIMON & SCHUSTER BOOKS FOR YOUNG READERS is a trademark of Simon & Schuster, Inc.
For information about special discounts for bulk purchases, please contact Simon & Schuster Special
Sales at 1-866-506-1949 or business@simonandschuster.com.
The Simon & Schuster Speakers Bureau can bring authors to your live event. For more information or
to book an event, contact the Simon & Schuster Speakers Bureau at 1-866-248-3049
or visit our website at www.simonspeakers.com.
Book design by Elizabeth Baddeley and Chloë Foglia
The text for this book was set in Caxon and hand lettered.
The illustrations for this book were rendered using a mix of traditional and digital media.
Manufactured in China • 0820 SCP
16 18 20 19 17 15
Library of Congress Cataloging-in-Publication Data
Levy, Debbie, author.
I dissent : Ruth Bader Ginsburg makes her mark / Debbie Levy ; illustrated by Elizabeth Baddeley.—
pages cm
ISBN 978-1-4814-6559-5 (hardcover)
ISBN 978-1-4814-6560-1 (eBook)
1. Ginsburg, Ruth Bader—Juvenile literature. 2. Judges—United States—Biography—Juvenile
literature. I. Baddeley, Elizabeth, illustrator. II. Title.
KF8745.G56L48 2016
347.73'2634—dc23
[B]
2015034756

I DISSENT

RUTH BADER GINSBURG MAKES HER MARK

written by
DEBBIE LEVY

illustrations by
ELIZABETH BADDELEY

Simon & Schuster Books for Young Readers
New York   London   Toronto   Sydney   New Delhi

You could say that Ruth Bader Ginsburg's life has been . . .
one disagreement after another.

DISAGREEMENT WITH CREAKY OLD IDEAS.

WITH **UNFAIRNESS.** WITH **INEQUALITY.**

RUTH HAS **DISAGREED, DISAPPROVED,** AND **DIFFERED.**

SHE HAS OBJECTED. SHE HAS RESISTED.

SHE HAS DISSENTED.

DISAGREEABLE? NO. DETERMINED? YES.

This is how Ruth Bader Ginsburg changed her life—and ours.

In 1940, little Ruth's neighborhood was vibrant with immigrants—people from Italy, Ireland, England, Poland, and Germany. Jews from Russia, like Ruth's father, Nathan Bader. People from different cultures with different holidays, foods, and traditions.

But in all these families in Brooklyn, New York, and in families everywhere, one thing was the same:

Boys were expected to grow up, go out in the world, and do big things.

Girls? Girls were expected to find husbands.

Celia Amster Bader thought girls should also have the chance to make their mark on the world. So she took Ruth to the library.

On the shelves were stories of girls and women who did big things. Ruth read about Nancy Drew, girl detective. She discovered Amelia Earhart, daring aviator. She learned of Athena, goddess of Greek myths. Here were independent girls and women, taking charge.

Ruth read her way into this world. Around her, the sweet scent of books blended with savory aromas from the Chinese restaurant downstairs. Delicious! A girl could be anything.

Sometimes Ruth and her parents took car trips out of the crowded city.
As they drove past a hotel in Pennsylvania, Ruth saw a sign:

This is how it was in those days: hotels, restaurants,
even entire neighborhoods announcing,

Ruth and her family were Jewish. This was prejudice, pure and simple.
Now it was Ruth's turn to disagree.
She disagreed by never forgetting how it felt to read such words.
She never forgot the sting of prejudice.

In elementary school, Ruth was excellent in some classes—and less excellent in others. Her favorites were English, history, and gym. In those, she did well.

But then there was handwriting. Ruth was left-handed. Back then, teachers told left-handers they should try to write with their right hands. Ruth's right-handed penmanship was so bad, she earned a D on her penmanship test.

She cried.

THEN SHE PROTESTED.

Ruth protested by writing with her left hand from that day forward. And it turned out she had quite nice handwriting!

Ruth also had a little problem with sewing and cooking. These were her least favorite classes—but girls had to take them. Boys took shop, where they worked with saws and other tools.

She wanted to take shop! She wanted to handle a saw!

She didn't get what she wanted. It may have been unfair to girls, and to boys, but Ruth was learning that sometimes life was like that.

Ruth loved music. She especially loved opera. In music class, she lifted her voice in song.

This time it was Ruth's music teacher who objected—gently. Ruth simply could not carry a tune. The teacher asked Ruth not to sing out loud in the chorus.

Ruth kept on singing—in the shower and in her dreams. She continued to adore opera, too.

By the time Ruth was in high school, friends and teachers knew her as an outstanding student, baton twirler, cello player, and newspaper editor. As graduation approached, Ruth was chosen to make a speech at the ceremony. But she had been keeping a big secret: Her mother was terribly sick. The day before graduation, Celia Bader died.

There was no agreeing with this. There was no disagreeing. This simply . . . was.
Ruth did not go to her graduation. She did not give her speech.
Still, Ruth knew what her mother wanted. Three months later, she left home to attend college.

Not many girls went to college in the 1950s. Ruth made friends, but she also met girls who excluded Jews from their clubs. She met boys who thought girls should be looking for husbands. And then she met Martin Ginsburg.

Marty was tall and funny. Ruth was small and serious. Marty could make her laugh. They fell in love and hatched a plan: After college, they would go to law school—both of them. Lawyers, Ruth had learned, could fight unfairness and prejudice in courts.

People thought it was a fine idea for Marty to attend law school. They didn't think Ruth should go. A lady lawyer? People disapproved.

RUTH DISAPPROVED RIGHT BACK.

SO DID MARTY.

They got married. They went to law school. And they had a baby—Jane.

Ruth's law school class had a total of nine women—and five hundred men. She studied mightily and tied for first place in the class. And yet at graduation time no one would hire this brilliant new lawyer.

Why not?

She was a woman. Men didn't want to work with a woman.

She was a mother. Men thought a mother wouldn't pay attention to work.

She was Jewish. Many people were (still) prejudiced.

Three strikes against her. But Ruth was not out.

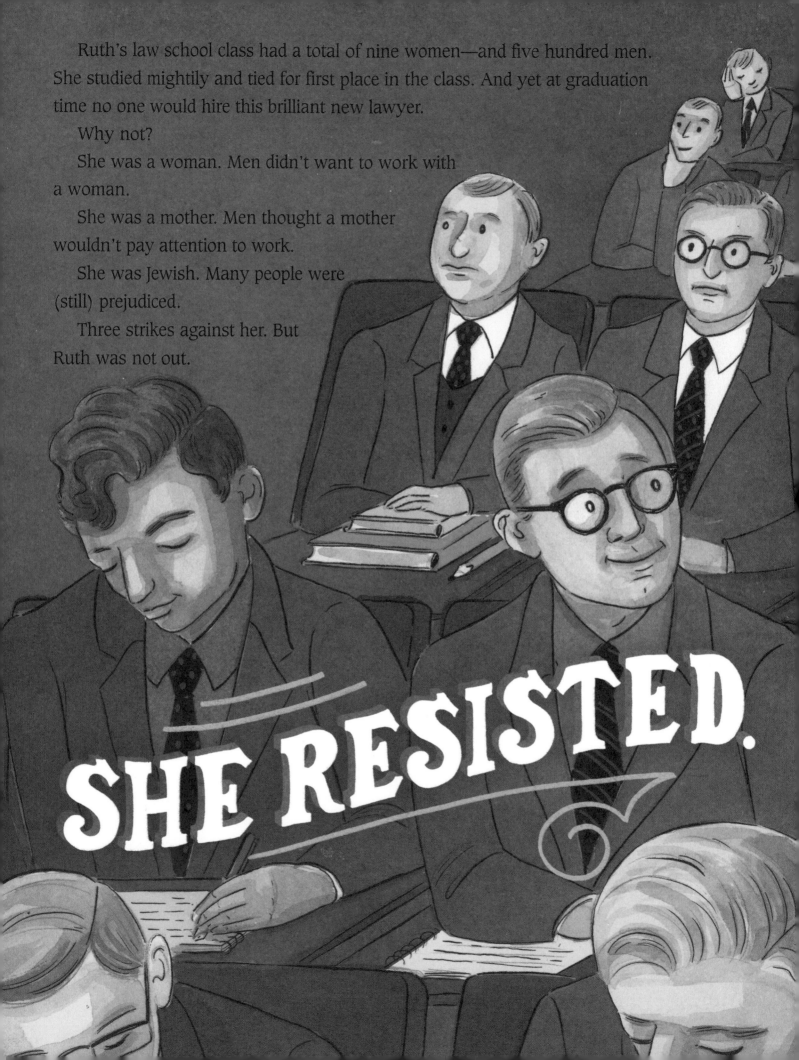

SHE RESISTED.

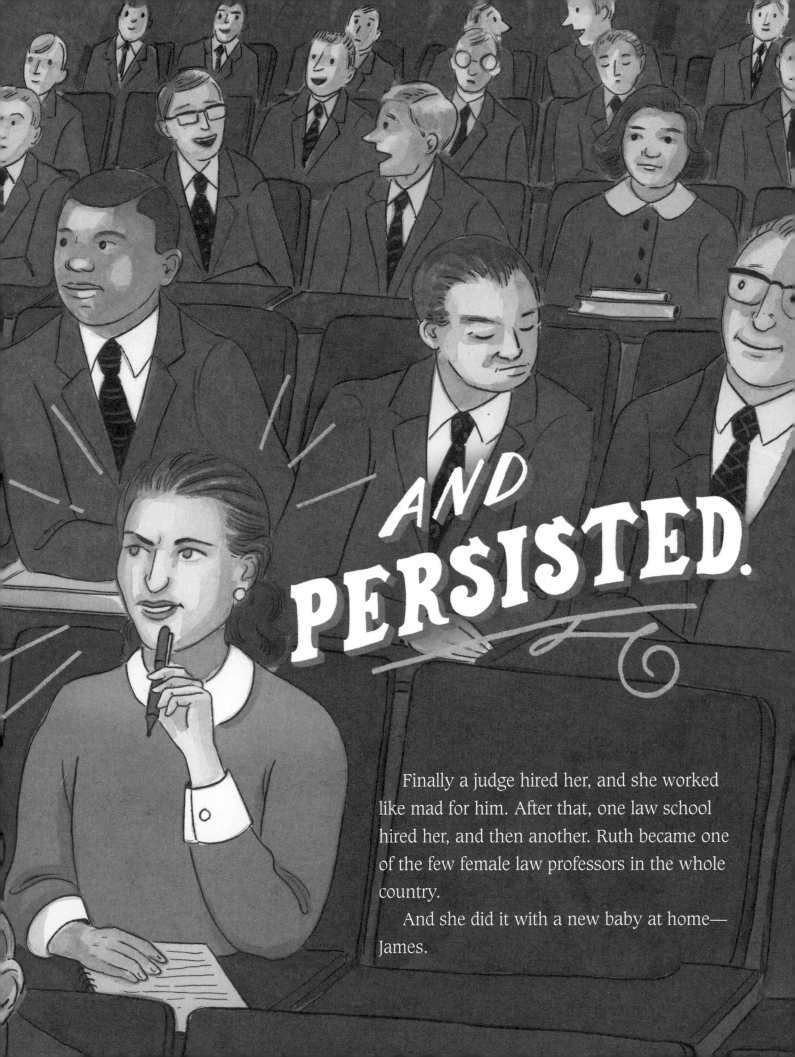

AND PERSISTED.

Finally a judge hired her, and she worked like mad for him. After that, one law school hired her, and then another. Ruth became one of the few female law professors in the whole country.

And she did it with a new baby at home—James.

Ruth had disagreed—and *worked*—her way into being a lawyer and professor. But around her, other women were excluded from jobs. When they did get jobs, they earned less than men. They were kept out of important roles in courts and government.

To make matters worse, the Supreme Court of the United States, the highest court in the land, approved all this. As one Supreme Court justice had written years before:

THE NATURAL AND PROPER **TIMIDITY** AND **DELICACY** WHICH BELONGS TO THE **FEMALE SEX** EVIDENTLY UNFITS IT FOR MANY OF THE OCCUPATIONS OF CIVIL LIFE.

In other words: Women and girls were too shy and weak to do big things in the world.

Another Supreme Court opinion declared:

WOMAN ~HAS ALWAYS~ **BEEN DEPENDENT** UPON MAN.

So Ruth went to court to fight for equal treatment of women.

The most important cases went to the Supreme Court. The first time she appeared there, Ruth was so nervous she feared she might be sick.

But standing before the nine Supreme Court justices, Ruth imagined them as her students. She, Professor Ginsburg, needed to teach these students—who were all men—why a person's choices shouldn't be limited just because she was born a girl.

Ruth wasn't only fighting for women. When women were excluded from the work world, men were excluded from home life. Why shouldn't a father stay home to care for his children and cook the meals? Why shouldn't his wife run a business? These were fresh ideas in the 1970s.

Ruth did not win every case, but she won enough. With each victory, women and men and girls and boys enjoyed a little more equality.

Sometimes Ruth and Marty's children received confused looks when they said that their mother argued cases in the Supreme Court and their father made the family's dinners. People found this strange.

RUTH, MARTY, JANE, AND JAMES DID NOT CONCUR.

They kept on being the type of family they wanted to be.

And dinners at the Ginsburg home were delicious! Marty was a successful lawyer, but also a marvelous chef who had mastered the art of French cooking.

Ruth, her family knew, had mastered the art of burnt pot roast.

Ruth became well known as a lawyer—so well known that President Jimmy Carter chose her to be a judge in Washington, DC.

Then Ruth became known as a first-rate judge—and President Bill Clinton asked her to be a justice on the Supreme Court. Along with the eight other Supreme Court justices, her job would be to decide the most significant cases and answer the most difficult legal questions in the United States.

RUTH AGREED.

In 1993, Justice Ruth Bader Ginsburg became the first Jewish woman on the nation's highest court.

In each case the Supreme Court considers, after hearing from lawyers who argue for each side, the nine justices take a vote. The side that gets the most votes wins the case. The justices who agree write an opinion to explain the court's ruling. When Justice Ginsburg votes with the winning side, she wears a special lace collar over her robe. But many times, when the Supreme Court announces the decision . . .

Justice Ginsburg disagrees.

she says, and she writes her own opinion explaining why.
Plus, she wears a different collar, just for dissenting.

I DISSENT,

Justice Ginsburg said when the court wouldn't help women or African Americans or immigrants who had been treated unfairly at work.

I DISSENT,

when the court rejected a law meant to protect the right of all citizens to vote, no matter their skin color.

I DISSENT,

when the court said no to schools that offered African Americans a better chance to go to college.

Justice Ginsburg can be very convincing. In one dissent, she explained why the court was wrong to rule against women workers who were fighting to get paid the same as men. Congress and the president agreed with her and passed a law to undo the court's ruling.

Justice Ginsburg has disagreed most often with the legal views of Justice Antonin Scalia. But they *didn't* just complain:

They shared their conflicting ideas. Each pointed out weaknesses in the other's arguments. And after the opinions were written . . .

the two justices had fun with each other! They didn't let disagreements about law get in the way of a long friendship.

Parasailing in France

Riding an elephant in India

Justice Ginsburg is now the oldest member of the Supreme Court. Some people have said she should quit because of her age.

Justice Ginsburg begs to differ.

She works as hard as ever. She exercises in the gym. She never misses a day in court. She attends the opera, gives speeches, and travels.

Many have cheered Justice Ginsburg for her persistence and independence. They've called her a rock star, a queen, a goddess—a hero!

Of course, Ruth Bader Ginsburg isn't a rock star, a queen, or a goddess.

But to many, she is a hero.

She made change happen, and she changed minds.

She cleared a path for people to follow in her footsteps—girls in college, women in law school, and everyone who wants to be treated without prejudice.

Her voice may not carry a tune, but it sings out for equality.

Step by step, she has made a difference . . .

ONE DISAGREEMENT AFTER ANOTHER

More About Ruth Bader Ginsburg

Not so many years ago most people believed that women were less capable than men of being leaders, making important decisions, and working in business and government. Women were encouraged to do three things: find husbands, have children, and keep house. At the same time people believed that men were ill-suited to take care of children. This was the world in which Ruth Bader Ginsburg grew up in the 1930s and 1940s.

These limitations continued into the 1950s, 1960s, and 1970s, although with some changes. More women entered the world of work than they had in earlier times, but in limited roles. A woman could become a teacher or a nurse or an airline attendant. She was far less likely to become a college professor or a doctor or an airline pilot.

But there were always some people who bristled at these limitations. The fight for equality had begun decades before, led by people such as Susan B. Anthony (1820–1906), Elizabeth Cady Stanton (1815–1902), Harriet Tubman (*circa* 1820–1913), Sojourner Truth (*circa* 1797–1883), and others. And this fight was carried on by Ruth Bader Ginsburg.

Ruth was born on March 15, 1933, in Brooklyn, New York. Ruth's father, Nathan Bader, worked in the clothing business, making and selling fur coats and hats. Celia Amster Bader, Ruth's mother, took care of home and family. With her forward-looking ideas about what girls and women could do, and her love of learning and reading, Celia Bader had a profound influence on Ruth's life. Ruth later called her a woman of "tremendous intellect" and "the bravest and strongest person I have known."

Sadly, Celia Bader died the day before Ruth graduated from high school in June 1950. This wasn't the first time the Bader family had faced tragedy. Ruth had had an older sister, Marilyn, who had died when Ruth was still a baby.

When her mother died, Ruth was devastated. But she knew her mother wanted her to continue with her education. So three months after Celia Bader's death, Ruth entered Cornell University, in Ithaca, New York. At first she didn't have clear goals about a career. But this was the 1950s, a time

when some leaders in the United States—a U.S. senator named Joseph McCarthy in particular—were threatening the rights of citizens to think and speak independently. Senator McCarthy believed that people who didn't share his beliefs about government needed to be silenced and even imprisoned. From one of her professors at Cornell, Ruth learned that lawyers could fight back. Lawyers could also fight the type of prejudice she had discovered when she'd seen that sign outside a hotel, NO DOGS OR JEWS ALLOWED.

In 1956 Ruth enrolled in law school. She started at Harvard Law School in Cambridge, Massachusetts, and later transferred to Columbia Law School in New York City. These are two of the best law schools in the country. Despite her stellar performance, Ruth struggled in 1959 to find a job after graduation, until Judge Edmund Palmieri of New York agreed to give her a try. Her abilities soon became clear to the judge and to other lawyers. Law firms had refused to hire her before; now they came to her with job offers. But Ruth's interest had turned toward teaching, and she became one of the first female law professors in the country, first at Rutgers School of Law in Newark, New Jersey (starting in 1963), and then at Columbia Law School (in 1972).

It was while she was a law professor that Ruth became involved in the fight for equality. She worked with the American Civil Liberties Union, a group whose mission is to protect freedoms guaranteed by the United States Constitution and laws. The Constitution is the highest law in the country. It sets out our basic rights and system of government in broad terms. Disagreements about what the Constitution means are resolved by courts—including, as a final resort, the Supreme Court of the United States.

Lawyers can't simply walk into a courtroom and announce that they intend to fight unfairness or uphold rights. Under our legal system, a lawyer represents a person—a client—who has been harmed in some way. The lawyer brings a lawsuit, or case, complaining of the wrong to the client. Ruth represented both women and men who had been harmed by rules and restrictions that treated women and men differently for no good reason.

In 1973 Ruth argued her first case before the Supreme Court. That case—when Ruth was so nervous that she feared she might be sick—was for a woman, Sharron Frontiero, who worked for the United States Air Force in a military hospital. Air force officers who were men automatically received benefits for their wives, such as payments for their wives' visits to doctors and dentists. But female officers, like Sharron Frontiero, didn't get those same automatic payments for their husbands. Frontiero's lawyers, including Ruth, argued that this exclusion was not permissible under the Constitution. The Constitution says that every person has a right to equal protection of the laws, and the air force was treating Frontiero and other women unequally without any good reason.

When Sharron Frontiero won that case, it wasn't just a victory for Sharron and other women in the air force. It was a victory for everyone seeking equality between men and women. As a result of this case and others that Ruth argued, the Supreme Court created guidelines for whenever the government treats men and women differently. If the government wishes to apply rules one way to men and another way to women, the Supreme Court said, it must have a very good reason.

Later Ruth explained her role as a lawyer fighting for equality in this way:

"I was trying to educate the judges that there was something wrong with the notion, 'Sugar and spice and everything nice, that's what little girls are made of'—for that very notion was limiting the opportunities, the aspirations of our daughters."

In 1980, after seventeen years of teaching law and winning cases in courts around the country, Ruth became Judge Ruth Bader Ginsburg of the United States Court of Appeals for the District of Columbia Circuit. She and her family moved to Washington, DC. Then, thirteen years later, in 1993, Judge Ginsburg became Justice Ginsburg of the Supreme Court of the United States, also in the nation's capital. She was the first Jewish woman and second woman to become a justice.

(Sandra Day O'Connor was the first female justice, appointed in 1981.)

As a judge and justice, Ruth could no longer represent clients. But she has continued to work for fairness and equality through her judicial opinions. One of her proudest moments came three years after she joined the Supreme Court. In that year the justices heard a case challenging the exclusion of girls from Virginia Military Institute (VMI), a famous state college dedicated to educating "citizen-soldiers." The college said that allowing girls to attend VMI would "destroy" the school.

Justice Ginsburg disagreed with VMI. She believed that if girls could handle the course of study and tough physical requirements demanded by VMI, they should have the opportunity to go there. Excluding girls, she believed, violated their right to equal protection under the Constitution.

But Justice Ginsburg did not have to dissent in the case—because six other justices also disagreed with the school. Justice Ginsburg wrote the opinion for the Supreme Court, ruling that VMI could not exclude girls. Women today, she wrote, "count as citizens in our American democracy equal in stature to men." She could have said that this equal stature was thanks in large part to her work as a lawyer—but she didn't mention that. She simply and clearly read a summary of the opinion out loud in the courtroom, making another mark for equality.

Notes on Supreme Court Cases

The name of the first case that Professor Ruth Bader Ginsburg argued in the Supreme Court is *Frontiero v. Richardson* (1973). Other cases she argued before the Supreme Court were *Kahn v. Shevin* (1974), *Weinberger v. Wiesenfeld* (1975), *Edwards v. Healy* (1975), *Califano v. Goldfarb* (1977), and *Duren v. Missouri* (1979).

The cases referred to in this book in which Justice Ginsburg dissented are: *Ledbetter v. Goodyear Tire & Rubber Co.* (2007), *Fisher v. University of Texas at Austin* (2013), *Vance v. Ball State University* (2013), *University of Texas Southwestern Medical Center v. Nassar* (2013), and *Shelby County v. Holder* (2013).

The VMI case referred to is *United States v. Virginia* (1996).

You can listen to audio recordings of the hearings, or oral arguments, at the Supreme Court on the Internet. The official Supreme Court website contains audio files and transcripts of hearings going back to 2010. The audio and transcript of the oral arguments in the voting rights case mentioned in this book (*Shelby County v. Holder*), for example, are at www.supremecourt.gov/oral_arguments/audio/2012/12-96. To hear the arguments in one of the workplace discrimination cases (*Vance v. Ball State University*), go to www.supreme-court.gov/oral_arguments/audio/2012/11-556. These are both cases in which Justice Ginsburg participated in questioning the lawyers appearing before the court.

To hear Professor Ruth Bader Ginsburg in her first argument before the Supreme Court—*Frontiero v. Richardson*—go to the website maintained by the Chicago-Kent College of Law, www.oyez.org, and navigate to www.oyez.org/cases/1972/71-1694.

Selected Bibliography

Books

* Eleanor H. Ayer. *Ruth Bader Ginsburg: Fire and Steel on the Supreme Court.* New York: Dillon Press (A People in Focus Book), 1994.

* Linda Bayer. *Ruth Bader Ginsburg.* Philadelphia: Chelsea House Publishers (Women of Achievement), 2000.

Scott Dodson, ed. *The Legacy of Ruth Bader Ginsburg.* New York: Cambridge University Press, 2015.

* Malka Drucker, illustrated by Elizabeth Rosen. *Portraits of Jewish-American Heroes.* New York: Dutton Children's Books, 2008.

Lynn Gilbert and Gaylen Moore. *Particular Passions: Talks with Women Who Have Shaped Our Times.* New York: C. N. Potter: Distributed by Crown, 1981.

Brian Lamb, Susan Swain, and Mark Farkas, eds. *The Supreme Court: A C-SPAN Book Featuring the Justices in Their Own Words.* New York: Public Affairs, 2010.

* Paul McCaffrey. *Ruth Bader Ginsburg: U.S. Supreme Court Justice.* New York: Chelsea House Publishers (Women of Achievement), 2010.

Elinor Porter Swiger. *Women Lawyers at Work.* New York: Julian Messner, 1978.

* Indicates books for young readers

Articles, Papers, Reports, and Interviews

Ruth Bader Ginsburg. "The Role of Dissenting Opinions." *Minnesota Law Review*, volume 95:1, 2010.

Ruth Bader Ginsburg Papers, 1897–2005. Library of Congress.

John Hockenberry. "Interview with Supreme Court Justice Ruth Bader Ginsburg." *The Takeaway*, www.thetakeaway.org/story/transcript-interview-justice-ruth-bader-ginsburg, September 16, 2013.

Nomination of Ruth Bader Ginsburg, to Be Associate Justice of the Supreme Court of the United States, Hearings before the Committee on the Judiciary, United States Senate, 103rd Congress, 1st Session, July 20, 21, 22, and 23, 1993. Washington, DC: U.S. Government Printing Office, 1994.

Jeffrey Rosen. "The New Look of Liberalism on the Court." *The New York Times Magazine*, October 5, 1997.

"The Stein Lecture: A Conversation Between Justice Ruth Bader Ginsburg and Professor Robert A. Stein." *Minnesota Law Review*, volume 99:1, 2014.

Jeffrey Toobin. "Heavyweight: How Ruth Bader Ginsburg Has Moved the Supreme Court." *The New Yorker*, March 11, 2013.

Video

Academy of Achievement. *Ruth Bader Ginsburg Interview.* www.achievement.org/autodoc/page/gin0int-1, August 17, 2010.

C-SPAN. *Justice Ginsburg Grade School Tour.* www.c-span.org/video/?57503-1/justice-ginsburg-grade-school-tour, June 3, 1994. [One year after Justice Ginsburg joined the Supreme Court, she visited her elementary school in Brooklyn, New York. She made a speech and took questions from students.]

Quotation Sources

"No dogs or Jews . . ." *Nomination of Ruth Bader Ginsburg*, page 139.

"The natural and proper timidity . . ." Supreme Court Justice Joseph P. Bradley, writing his own opinion, *Bradwell v. Illinois*, 83 U.S. 130 (1873).

"Woman has always . . ." Supreme Court Justice David J. Brewer, writing the unanimous opinion, *Muller v. Oregon*, 208 U.S. 412 (1908).

"tremendous intellect" Swiger, *Women Lawyers at Work*, page 55.

"the bravest and strongest . . ." "The Supreme Court: Transcript of President's Announcement and Judge Ginsburg's Remarks," *The New York Times*, June 15, 1993.

"I was trying . . ." *Nomination of Ruth Bader Ginsburg*, page 122.

"citizen-soldiers," "destroy," "count as citizens . . ." *United States v. Virginia*, 518 U.S. 515 (1996).

Book jacket, "Fight for the things . . ." Ruth Bader Ginsburg, Remarks at Radcliffe Day Celebration, May 29, 2015.